MUNICIPAL BUSES IN LANCASHIRE

by

Andrew Wiltshire

One of Hyndburn's Leyland PD3As with 70-seat bodies from East Lancashire Coachbuilders in nearby Blackburn is seen heading through Accrington on 16 July 1975. This bus, 162 (9690 TJ) was numerically the last of five similar vehicles delivered to Accrington Corporation Transport between March 1962 and November 1963. The initial three (158 to 160) were PD3A/1 models with manual synchromesh gearboxes, while 161 and the subject of this view were PD3A/2 models with pneumocyclic semi-automatic transmission. These Leylands followed the delivery in 1961 of a pair of unique 28-foot rear entrance Guy Wulfrunians, which had a relatively short life in Accrington. Guys however were back in favour in 1964, when the fairly new Arab V model was introduced in the form of three East Lancs-bodied examples, the last rear entrance buses to enter the fleet.

(John Jones)

Introduction

Lancashire, once much larger than it is today, is a fascinating and diverse area, that is steeped in history. There can be few counties in the United Kingdom that were as colourful and interesting as Lancashire, when it came to bus operations. The municipal contribution in the 1960s was no exception, with twenty-seven fleets, offering a wealth of interesting vehicles with many individual and familiar livery styles. This would all change significantly from the late 1960s onwards.

Without a doubt the most common make of vehicle in the Lancashire municipal sector was the Leyland. However, amongst the sea of Leylands were many other manufacturers such as Guy, Crossley, AEC and Daimler to name just some. The county was also home to a number of major bodybuilders, and municipal operators were not shy to support local industry. Although not Lancashire-based, the fleets of Stockport Corporation and the SHMD Board have been included, as they played an important part in municipal bus operation in the county. The creation of SELNEC PTE (South East Lancashire North East Cheshire Passenger Transport Executive) would spell the end for eleven municipal fleets.

This book begins its journey in the 1960s, and sets out to illustrate these municipal fleets and a selection of the vehicles they operated since then. I have tried to identify some of the significant events, a number of which occurred as a result of political changes to the county, whilst others marked periods of intense competition between operators large and small. Whatever the outcome, the result is that in 2011, Lancashire has only two municipal fleets still operating within its boundaries. The pages of this book will hopefully give you the chance to appreciate the much-loved liveries and some of the vehicles that have now sadly been consigned to history.

Acknowledgements

Researching this book over the past year has further enhanced my knowledge of this area and has brought much pleasure. I have learnt a great deal and made some new and valued acquaintances along the way. A very large thank you must go to John Jones, David Beilby and Cliff Essex for the time and effort which they have given to this project.

I must thank John, and many others for providing me with a superb selection of images, which hopefully give this title the special quality it deserves. Without the help of Chris Aston (Omnicolour), Cliff Essex, David Beilby, Malcolm Keeley, Claire Pendrous, Les Simpson, Arthur Day and John Wiltshire, the book would not have advanced beyond first gear. Also many thanks to Pete Brabham and my wife Tracey, for bringing a number of elderly images back to life with their digital skills.

As always, thanks must go out to my colleagues at the Wythall Transport Museum for their continued support and interest in my publications. Written sources used throughout include copies of Ian Allan British Bus Fleets, Capital Transport and British Bus Publishing Bus Handbooks, PSV Circle fleet histories and a number of publications dedicated to municipal fleets in the Lancashire area. I must also thank the staff of Amadeus Press for their continued excellence in the production of a fine book.

Andrew Wiltshire - Cardiff, February 2011

Published by Bernard McCall, 400 Nore Road, Portishead, Bristol, BS20 8EZ, England. Website : www.coastalshipping.co.uk. Telephone/fax : 01275 846178. E-mail : bernard@coastalshipping.co.uk. All distribution enquiries should be addressed to the publisher.

Printed by Amadeus Press, Ezra House, West 26 Business Park, Cleckheaton, West Yorkshire, BD19 4TQ. Telephone : 01274 863210; fax : 01274 863211. E-mail : info@amadeuspress.co.uk; website : www.amadeuspress.co.uk

ISBN : 978-1-902953-52-6

Front cover: In the years following World War 2 Wigan's bus fleet was entirely of Leyland manufacture, and the bodywork for its vehicles was also sourced locally. Northern Counties was Wigan-based and so was Massey, located to the south-west of the town in Pemberton, while Leyland was only eleven miles to the north. All post-war double-deckers were Leyland Titans until 1969, when the first Atlanteans arrived. Single-deckers were purchased only in small numbers, and consisted of Royal Tigers and later both Panther Cub and Panther models. On a fine day in March 1966 we see Leyland PD2 number 114 (CEK 837) pulling out of Parson's Walk and passing the civic buildings in Wigan town centre. It has a Northern Counties body and dates from 1956.

(Martin Llewellyn - Omnicolour)

Back cover: Preston Corporation's crimson and cream livery gave way to a new blue and ivory colour scheme in 1967, following livery experiments the previous year (see page 33). Preston had taken its first Leyland PD2s in 1950, a large batch of twenty PD2/1 models with Leyland 56-seat bodies. Further examples of the Leyland PD2 model followed in the years to 1957. Number 48 (ECK 508) was one of eight Leyland PD2/10s delivered in 1952 and numbered 41 to 48. It is seen heading east out of Preston on its way to Farringdon Park early one morning in March 1967, and wearing the new blue and ivory livery. Road traffic is sparse, and the trees are still devoid of any leaves as spring approaches. For many years Preston Corporation did not use route numbers but rather route letters which were derived from an abbreviation of the out-of-town terminus, a practice which ceased in 1980. Number 48 was to see nearly twenty years service, not being withdrawn until January 1972.

(Omnicolour)

A wealth of colour and variety.

In the 1960s, Lancashire's municipal fleets continued to offer the enthusiast an immense variety of vehicle types and liveries. A sense of civic pride and professionalism still prevailed in fleets both large and small. After Manchester and Salford, Bolton had the largest municipal fleet in the Greater Manchester area. It was a committed Leyland user, and unusually, from the early post-war years, most buses had air brakes. It was predominantly a double-deck fleet, and after 1933 had no low bridge restrictions, therefore requiring only a handful of single-deckers. Four Crossley saloons arrived in 1949 and an East Lancs-bodied Leyland Royal Tiger with air brakes entered the fleet as number 9 in 1955. A similar, but vacuum-braked vehicle took fleet number 10 in 1956, which had originally been ordered as a Tiger Cub. It had bodywork by Bond. It is seen on 7 May 1970 pulling into Breightmet Street, close to Shiffnall Street garage where the single-deckers were based. On paper it is at this date technically a SELNEC PTE bus. However, to the observer it still looks every bit a Bolton bus.

(Cliff Essex)

The operation of the tramways in Bolton finally ceased in March 1947, having been replaced by seventy-five Crossleys delivered in 1946/47, numbered 246 to 320. Replacement of the pre-war bus fleet saw forty Leyland PD1s arrive in 1947 followed by one hundred Leyland PD2s in 1948/49, which were all air-braked PD2/4 models. The first fifty arrived in 1948 and included 356 (CWH 706) which we see off service at the bus park near Bolton's old bus station in June 1969. All one hundred buses had 8 feet wide Leyland bodies with seating for 56 passengers, later increased to 58. The next new buses were not received until 1955, when delivery of Leylands resumed, though in the 1957 to 1961 period, these were interspersed with thirty-six Daimler CVG6s and six AEC Regent Vs. Number 356 was withdrawn shortly after this view was taken and passed with the Bolton fleet to SELNEC PTE, but as a withdrawn vehicle.

(Cliff Essex)

Twenty-one Daimler CVG6 chassis with preselector gearboxes were specified for 1957, which raised a few eyebrows locally as Leyland had been in favour for some time. The initial ten, numbered 85 to 94, would have East Lancs bodies with platform doors, like 90 (KWH 570) seen here in March 1965. Metro-Cammell would supply bodies for the remaining eleven buses which became 95 to 105, and these had traditional open platforms and seating for 62 passengers. In 1958 a further seven CVG6s were received (106 to112), but this time were thirty feet in length and seated 74. In 1960 Mr Ralph Bennett took over as general manager and experimented with a red and cream livery. However, Bolton's maroon was retained but with a larger application of cream, as worn by number 90 in this view. Bolton Transport Department had three garages, the newest being Crook Street which opened in 1929.

(Martin Llewellyn - Omnicolour)

Bury is located five miles to the east of Bolton and famous for, amongst other things, the open-air market and its black pudding dish. The Corporation's main bus depot was on Rochdale Road and, having previously been red and white until 1943, its buses were then painted in a pleasing apple green and deep primrose livery with dark green wings. The largest single batch of buses ever purchased by Bury Corporation comprised twenty-five much-loved Weymann-bodied Leyland PD3/6s, delivered between April 1958 and March 1959, all fitted with platform doors. Having acquired Leyland Atlanteans and Daimler Fleetlines, the latter in both double and single-deck form, in 1967 Bury purchased four further half-cabs. These East Lancs-bodied PD2s were specially obtained for route 23T, the more direct service between Bury and Bolton, which had a weight restriction at Trinity Street station in Bolton. Here number 188 (FEN 588E) is seen close to Kay Gardens, Bury, in September 1967.

(Cliff Essex)

When Bury Corporation ordered a Guy Wulfrunian, unlike all other Wulfrunian customers, they had not hitherto purchased any Guy double-deckers. Maybe the attraction of its revolutionary design, coupled with the high seating capacity, prompted an order to be placed. The front-mounted Gardner 6LX engine, all round disc brakes and air-suspension at both front and rear, gave Bury a vehicle quite unlike any other municipal bus in the Manchester area. Numbered 101 (LEN 101), it had a 73-seat Roe body with Park Royal badges and appeared at the 1960 Commercial Motor Show as the first municipal example of a Wulfrunian. Taken into stock in December 1960, the bus was nicknamed Lenny but was sold after only three years in October 1963, having proved to be rather unsuccessful. It then moved to Wales, passing initially to Howells and Withers in Monmouthshire and moving north to Wright of Penycae near Wrexham in 1964. This nearside view in January 1962 provides a fascinating study of a remarkable vehicle.

(Cliff Essex collection)

Post-war double-deckers for Bury Corporation Transport included buses of Crossley, AEC and Leyland manufacture, with Weymann bodywork finding favour from 1947 until 1959. In 1963 Bury received its first rear engine buses, a batch of fifteen 75-seat Metro-Cammell-bodied Leyland Atlanteans numbered 102 to 116. The following year, a similar number of Alexander-bodied Daimler Fleetlines were delivered. These were the only such combination with a Lancashire municipal fleet, and one of them, 129 (TEN 129), is seen in Howell Croft South bus station in Bolton in March 1965. These attractive buses had Gardner 6LX engines and seated 74 passengers, and were followed in 1965 by half a dozen with equally smart looking East Lancs bodywork. The last new buses for Bury, all delivered in 1969, were three Leyland Atlantean double-deckers, six Daimler Fleetline saloons, and finally a small Bedford J2 bus which was for the Chesham Road route. Number 129 became SELNEC PTE number 6329.

(Martin Llewellyn - Omnicolour)

Rochdale lies in the valley of the River Roch, just under eleven miles to the north of Manchester. Motor buses first appeared in 1926 and a blue and cream livery was adopted in 1935, the well-known "streamlined" variation first appearing two years later, and this lasted until 1961. Unlike most of the operators in this book, Rochdale was a keen AEC user and bought a large number of Regent IIIs, and a handful of Regal IV under-floor engine saloons up to 1953. The initial batch of Regals of 1951 totalled seven buses, numbered 301 to 307. They had East Lancs bodywork with a front entrance and rear exit, and were not very economical on fuel. Seen in the centre of Rochdale in April 1968, is HDK 707, by now renumbered 7, and converted to single door layout seating 44 passengers. It was withdrawn in 1969 ending its days working in Northern Ireland.

(Cliff Essex)

Rochdale Corporation Transport made a temporary switch to Daimlers in 1953/54 when thirty CVG6s with Weymann bodywork arrived. A change of general manager in 1954 saw a return to AEC in 1956, with delivery of a batch of forty Regent V models numbered 268 to 307. These were fine looking buses with Weymann bodies, and were rather unusual in that they were fitted with the Gardner 6LW power unit, the only operator outside Scotland to specify such a combination. The first thirty buses, up to 297, had air-operated pre-selector gearboxes, the only Regent Vs built as such, while the remaining ten had monocontrol semi-automatic gearboxes. Number 284 (NDK 984) is seen at the garage in Mellor Street in September 1961 wearing the attractive monestral blue and cream livery for which Rochdale will always be remembered. The fleet strength at Rochdale in 1966 stood at 151 motor buses.

(Cliff Essex collection)

Rochdale introduced spray-painting of its buses in 1961 and one result of this was a simplified livery. AEC saloons returned to Rochdale in late 1961 with the arrival of five Reliances with Weymann 42-seat bodies featuring a centre exit. They were intended for one-man operation on routes 5 and 7/7A, and were also the first buses delivered new in the revised livery. The first of the batch, 16 (2116 DK), is seen in June 1962 on the Esplanade opposite Rochdale Town Hall, which dates from 1892.

Of note are the three glazed panels at roof level, a common feature at this time on saloons permitted to carry extra standing passengers. The AEC Reliance was a popular and economical chassis, and Rochdale added a further nine to its fleet before moving on to rear-engine saloons. The town of Rochdale would never be quite the same after its smart fleet of buses had passed to SELNEC PTE on 1 November 1969.

(Martin Llewellyn - Omnicolour)

Oldham is situated in the south-east corner of Lancashire, lying amongst the southern Pennine hills, and standing at around 700 feet above sea level. During the 1930s numerous Leyland Titan and Tiger models were delivered, with the majority of bodywork coming from English Electric or Roe. Small numbers of Crossleys were also purchased in the early post-war period, as well as twenty-five Daimler CVD6. All of these Daimlers were originally due to receive Crossley bodies, but in the event the first ten were completed in 1948 with smart looking 56-seat Roe bodywork. One of the Crossley-bodied examples was 329 (EBU 929), new in 1949, which is seen here towards end of its career parked in the yard of Oldham's garage, in what is believed to be late 1964. This bus had recently acquired an engine and, as seen here, a chrome-plated radiator, both from a Birmingham Corporation Daimler. Number 329 was withdrawn in 1966 and sold for scrap.

(Cliff Essex collection)

The first Leyland PD2 for Oldham arrived in 1948 and was a PD2/3 model, 26 feet long and 8 feet wide, Oldham being an early pioneer of the 8 feet wide bus. By the mid-1950s, the longer PD2/20 and PD2/30 models with tin fronts were specified, with bodywork from Roe, Northern Counties, Metro-Cammell and Crossley. A 1957 example is 402 (NBU 502) with classic Roe bodywork, seen here in September 1963. It has been parked adjacent to the Corporation bus garage at Wallshaw Street, and has just been repainted into an experimental two-tone blue livery.

The upper-works were described as peacock blue while the darker shade was garter blue. This attractive scheme would be modified further the following month, by taking the darker shade to above the lower deck windows, and above this adding an off-white band. It was not deemed a success and in 1966, number 402 would have one final claim to fame as the first half-cab to receive the new pommard and Devon cream livery.

(Cliff Essex collection)

In 1958/59 Oldham Corporation took delivery of its final batch of ten PD2s, with bodies from Wigan-based Northern Counties. After this, there was a five-year gap before the arrival of the last half-cabs, ten 30 feet Leyland PD3s with exposed radiators and Roe forward entrance bodywork, numbered 101 to 110. The year 1964 also saw the entry into service of four Marshall-bodied Leyland Tiger Cubs. From 1965 Oldham started to purchase Leyland Atlanteans, which were to become the standard double-deck bus for the next five years. The first ten examples had Roe bodywork to a very distinctive design with peaked roof domes, and the familiar engine "bustle" was disguised by the use of shrouds to give a very clean profile. A 1966 example of this body is 146 (GBU 146D), seen here at the top of Clegg Street near Oldham Town Hall most probably in 1967. It is wearing the pommard and cream livery and is on service V, which was an extended circular route. Number 146 was an exhibit at the 1966 Commercial Motor Show at Earl's Court and as a consequence carried the Leyland "wheel" badge below the fleet number on the front dash. The fleet stood at 180 buses when it passed to SELNEC PTE, of which 164 were double-deckers.

(David Beilby collection)

The town of Ashton-under-Lyne lies on the north bank of the River Tame and was historically renowned for important industries such as coal mining, iron production and numerous mills engaged in textile manufacturing. Motor buses first appeared in 1923, with the first trolleybuses arriving two years later, when the rundown of the tramway commenced, a task completed in 1938. The first double-deckers were four Crossley Condors in 1932, and these were followed by eighteen Crossley Mancunian models and seven Leyland TD5s in the years to 1939. In the late 1930s, the trolleybus system expanded including a number of routes running into the centre of Manchester. World War 2 saw no less than sixteen Massey-bodied Guy Arabs arrive, and from 1950 onwards, all apart from 72 and 74 were rebodied by Crossley. These two received elegant new Roe bodies in 1955 and went on to give a further eleven years service. Number 74 (FTE 891) is seen looking very smart in August 1964.

(Cliff Essex collection)

In the early post-war years Ashton-under-Lyne purchased half a dozen Crossley DD42 double-deckers followed by three Leyland PD1s all with Crossley bodywork. The first of many Leyland PD2s arrived in 1950, though four Guy Arab IVs with rare Bond bodywork were received in 1956. The same year saw the arrival of the last trolleybuses, eight BUTs, also with attractive Bond bodies, which survived until the closure of the system in 1966. Typical of two dozen attractive Roe-bodied Leyland PD2/40s delivered between 1960 and 1964 is 25 (225 YTB), seen in Ashton bus station in June 1968. Of interest is that the name of the general manager in post, Peter Bland, appears below the coat of arms on the upper deck of the bus. The last new buses for this fleet were a pair of East Lancs-bodied Panther Cubs in 1967 and five Leyland Atlanteans bodied by Northern Counties in 1969.

(Cliff Essex)

Prior to 1954 the Ashton livery had been a very distinctive dark blue with white and red relief, but this was to give way to a very attractive peacock blue and cream. The Corporation purchased four Leyland Tiger TS8 saloons in 1939 numbered 33 to 36. They had 36-seat Leyland bodywork and for a period during the war years received perimeter seating. Number 36 (DTE 324) had its bus seats removed in 1952, and 26 coach-type seats fitted for use on private hire and as the Committee Coach. As a result it outlived the other three Tigers which were withdrawn in 1956, and it continued in its new role until 1962 after which it was scrapped. It is seen here at the Mossley Road depot, still looking fairly presentable at the end of its life. Sixty buses passed with the Ashton-under-Lyne Corporation fleet to SELNEC PTE in November 1969.

(Cliff Essex collection)

The full title for this undertaking was The Stalybridge, Hyde, Mossley and Dukinfield Transport and Electricity Board; it was a Joint Board. SHMD Board was for many years the fleetname to be found on the side of its green and cream buses. Prior to 1974 the towns of Hyde, Dukinfield and Stalybridge were in Cheshire, while that of Mossley once spanned Cheshire, Lancashire and Yorkshire, until it became a Lancashire borough in 1885. Daimlers were the staple choice of chassis for many years, but there were exceptions. The innovative general manager Mr L G Stockwell introduced "standee" type saloons in 1952, initially on a Daimler Freeline and later Atkinson chassis. The only Atkinson double-decker ever completed entered service with SHMD in 1955. The first double-deckers with forward entrances were some Leyland PD2s in 1962, but a change of general manager saw Daimlers back in favour in 1964. One of these is number 9 (ATU 409B), seen in Ashton-under-Lyne in June 1969 and wearing the lighter shade of green introduced in 1957. All buses since 1950 had Northern Counties bodywork and number 9 seated 64 passengers.

(Cliff Essex)

Brush supplied bodies for ten Daimler CVD6 double-deckers in 1948, and a further departure from Northern Counties bodywork occurred in 1949, with the arrival of ten similar Daimlers with East Lancs bodies. These attractive buses, numbered 46 to 55, gave very good service and the whole batch lasted until 1968. In June 1967 number 54 (LMA 754) demonstrates the late style of fleet name, though the bus is starting to show its age as it takes a break in Hyde bus station. The SHMD garage in Tame Street, Stalybridge, featured an open-air parking ground, which opened in November 1962. This facility had provision for electrical heating of a vehicle's radiator and passenger saloons. Buses were parked in rows of five and in cold weather starting problems were theoretically avoided. The last new buses for SHMD were ten unusual short Daimler Fleetline double-deckers in 1968, whilst saloons consisted of six Bristol RESLs new in 1967. The SHMD fleet contributed eighty-seven buses to SELNEC PTE upon its formation.

(Martin Llewellyn - Omnicolour)

Stockport's buses were red and white, and immaculate in every respect. The fleet was always very smartly turned out, and its services were well run, a credit to its management. Stockport, although situated just inside Cheshire, ran services into Manchester and was also involved in joint operations with North Western Road Car and three municipal fleets, to destinations such as Ashton-under-Lyne, Hyde and Stalybridge. By the late 1960s the fleet was mostly made up of Leyland PD2 and PD3 models, and 348 (PJA 918) was one of ten PD2/30s received in 1960.

Stockport was by now unable to obtain bodywork from Leyland or Crossley and so Longwell Green of Bristol supplied bodies for this batch of buses, before a permanent switch was made to East Lancs from 1962. In June 1967 we see 348 in Ashton-under-Lyne bus station, which had been opened in November 1963.

(Cliff Essex)

The trolleybus first took to the streets in Manchester on 1 March 1938, when services to Ashton-under-Lyne and Stalybridge were introduced. Manchester Corporation employed a total of seventy-six new trolleybuses and a new garage was also built. From 1939 the network continued to expand taking in places such as Haughton Green, and also along the Rochdale and Oldham Roads. A further seventy-seven new trolleybuses were obtained during World War 2, and fifty-four Crossleys were delivered between 1949 and 1951. The Crossleys included sixteen three-axle Dominions, all with Crossley bodywork and seating for 66. A fine example is 1242 (JVU 747) seen taking a rest in Stockport Road, Hyde, in 1962, whilst on an enthusiasts' tour. Ironically, the gradual rundown of the trolleybus system began in 1955, the year in which the last trolleybuses were delivered, and the final service to run in Manchester was on 30 December 1966.

(A M Davies - Omnicolor)

Manchester Corporation Transport was a premier municipal undertaking and is the largest to be featured in this book, operating out of seven garages in 1966. Post-war double-deck buses were always Leylands and Daimlers, and also Crossleys until 1950. Saloons were very much in the minority at Manchester Corporation. The first Leyland PD2 models for this fleet were delivered from 1950, the initial batch having Leyland bodies. These were followed by sixty-five with Metro-Cammell bodywork like 3220 (JND 621) seen at work in this view. The date is March 1966 and the bus is on Cheetham Hill Road at Victoria Station. The body is to Manchester's standard post-war style, but has lost some of its character by the application of the revised livery with just a single cream band and a painted radiator.

(Cliff Essex)

Manchester received its first Daimler CVG6 models in 1950, a batch of ninety with traditional exposed radiators. The next examples arrived between 1953 and 1954 and comprised eighty buses (4400 to 4479) with Metro-Cammell 60-seat bodywork. They included 4437 (NNB 247) seen here in Piccadilly Gardens in March 1966. These buses had flush-fitted windows and the tin-front bonnet arrangement, which Manchester was forced to take as Daimler no longer offered the traditional exposed radiator. In 1965, the undertaking changed its title to Manchester City Transport, and in November 1969 all eighty Daimlers passed to SELNEC PTE.

(Cliff Essex)

The final vehicle developed for the Manchester undertaking was the Mancunian design. The Mancunian was a futuristic and stylish bus designed by general manager Ralph Bennett and his team specifically for one-man operation, and brought a new and much brighter livery to the streets of Manchester. The first examples were introduced from 1968, and comprised forty-eight Leyland Atlanteans and a similar number of Daimler Fleetlines, all with 73-seat dual-door bodywork from Park Royal, and would be the only short examples. Thereafter, longer 33-feet vehicles were introduced, and in subsequent batches, bodywork also came from Metro-Cammell-Weymann and East Lancs (only on Atlanteans). Number 1021 (HVM 921F) was one of the initial batch of Atlanteans and is seen travelling along Victoria Street, Manchester, in April 1968, the first month of operation of the type.

(Martin Llewellyn - Omnicolour)

Motor buses first appeared with Salford Corporation in 1920 and the trams were eventually ousted in 1947, supervised by a new general manager, Charles Baroth, who had arrived from Newport Corporation the previous year. Another very noticeable change would see the red and white livery change to green and cream with a silver roof. The Salford fleet had emerged from World War 2 in very poor shape with many pre-war buses needing major attention. The most cost-effective solution for this very run-down fleet was to replace as many buses as possible with new vehicles. In 1949 a substantial order was placed for 210 Daimler CVG6 chassis of which 195 would receive Metro-Cammell double-deck bodies, and the remaining fifteen would be delivered from Burlingham as saloons. In the event, 199 of them appeared as double-deckers, and took fleet numbers 351 to 440 and 452 to 560. Here we see 469 (FRJ 469), an example from the second batch of double-deckers, and new in 1951. It is photographed laying over in the Victoria bus station in Salford during March 1966, and would remain in service until 1969.

(Chris Aston - Omnicolour)

After the major post-war fleet renewal in the years up to 1952, no further buses were needed until 1962. The Salford fleet was now very smart and enhanced by the lack of advertising on its vehicles, a feature that was to remain until almost the end of operations in 1969. Ironically, the Leyland PD2 did not make its initial appearance in the Salford fleet until 1963, at around the time that it had finally fallen out of favour in the neighbouring Manchester fleet. Despite buying Leyland Titans in considerable numbers between 1963 and 1967, Salford tried a small quantity of rear engine Leyland Atlanteans and Daimler Fleetlines, before placing an order for twenty-one Atlanteans for delivery in 1964/65. The batch took fleet numbers 212 to 232, and 231 (DBA 231C) is seen in brand new condition on Victoria Bridge Street in March 1965. It has a Metro-Cammell body seating 76 passengers, and the front lower panel moulding emulates what is regarded as a Manchester Corporation style. A total of 271 Salford buses passed to SELNEC PTE along with the two bus garages at Frederick Road and Weaste.

(Chris Aston - Omnicolour)

Leigh was an industrial town twelve miles to the west of Manchester. It was well-known for cotton spinning and also had some coal mining, two of the well-known collieries being Bickershaw and Parsonage. Leigh Corporation only ever ran motor buses, and was not a large fleet but was always interesting and varied. The garage in Holden Road was occupied from the early 1930s, and was a former engineering works. It had low doorways, and was therefore unable to accommodate "full height" double-deckers. The first six Leyland PD2s for this fleet arrived in 1948 and featured Roberts bodywork, numbered 24 to 19 in descending order. They were followed in 1949 by ten with Lydney bodywork numbered between 7 and 18 in more conventional ascending order. The first of these, number 7 (KTD 759), is seen at the end of its career in 1969 parked at the rear of the Leigh garage, having just been withdrawn from service.

(Cliff Essex)

Not only did the height restriction at the garage dictate the use of low height double-deckers, but until the 1960s, the road network around Leigh had numerous low bridges. After receiving seven AEC Regents in 1952, Leigh returned to Leyland in 1955, placing an order for its first 8 feet wide buses. These comprised five PD2s with East Lancs bodywork and BMMO style full width bonnets. Despite the increased dimensions, these buses and three similar vehicles delivered in 1957 had seats for just 53 passengers. However, five more PD2s delivered later in 1957 seated a more useful 58, like number 55 (491 DTC) in this view. The bus is seen off its normal haunts, in Manchester's Lower Mosley Street bus station in June 1966. The 53-seaters were upgraded to 58 from 1961, and Leigh went on to become the first municipal customer for the Dennis Loline in 1958, and again for the AEC Renown from 1963. Fifty-seven buses passed to SELNEC's Northern Division in 1969.

(Cliff Essex)

The buses of Wigan Corporation were crimson and white and apart from six utilities received during World War 2, all buses since 1929 were of Leyland manufacture. Double-deckers always played a dominant role at Wigan Corporation Transport and the first Titans were received in 1929. Many PD2s were operated from 1950, the early examples having Leyland bodies after which the local concerns of Massey Bros and Northern Counties shared all the future orders. The first examples with "new look" tin-fronts arrived in 1956 and were PD2/20 models with Northern Counties bodywork (see cover). Similar models delivered the following year were three with Massey bodywork and platform doors, including number 2 (DEK 105). Wigan's fleet numbering system was for over fifty years a little unconventional, and was based upon allocating a vacant number to the next new vehicle, instead of using blocks of numbers. Number 2 is seen in August 1972 outside what was known as the Central Depot in Melverley Street, Wigan.

(Cliff Essex)

Motor bus operation in St Helens began on 17 August 1923 with two short routes in the hands of a single vehicle. The poor condition of much of the tramway resulted in the introduction of trolleybuses on certain tram routes from July 1927. Early motor buses were of Guy manufacture, but in the run up to World War 2 Leylands were favoured. Leyland PD2s were received from 1954, and the first nine were rare PD2/9 models with Davies bodies, for use on the Carr Mill service. The bus in this February 1966 view, F108 (EDJ 508), was however one of nineteen PD2/20s with East Lancs bodies, delivered in 1955 to 1957. Davies also bodied one PD2/20 in 1956 (F112) before leaving the bodybuilding business. F108 features the fleet number prefix which was introduced with these buses in 1955, and was perpetuated until 1965. This bus lasted with St. Helens for just twelve years before being sold in 1968 to Jones Motors of Ynysybwl near Pontypridd.

(Martin Llewellyn - Omnicolour)

Some of the first new vehicles for St. Helens after World War 2 were Bristol K6As with lowbridge bodies and eight Roe-bodied Bristol L6A saloons. Between 1948 and 1952, St. Helens received fifty-four AEC Regents including forty of the RT type, before Leyland returned to favour in 1954 (see above). Some joint services with Lancashire United and Ribble were established which took St. Helens buses to places such as Southport and Warrington. It was with this in mind that a solitary Roe-bodied AEC Regal IV was purchased in 1951, and which featured a two-door layout. This attractive bus was numbered 209 (BDJ 329) and was intended to be the first of several similar vehicles for use on the St. Helens to Southport route, which had a low bridge restriction. The bridge was soon replaced, and therefore 209 remained unique in the fleet. It is seen here at work in June 1962, and was finally retired in 1965, passing to a private operator in Hampshire.

(Martin Llewellyn - Omnicolour)

Southport is located on the Irish Sea coast about sixteen miles to the north of Liverpool. Historically, it was a refined seaside town with an impressive pier and much Victorian architecture. In 1947 Southport Corporation received some of the very first Leyland PD2s to be completed, and apart from several AECs and Crossleys received in 1949/50, this became the standard double-decker for many years. The last generation of front engine double-deckers to grace the streets of Southport were the forward entrance Leyland PD2s and in all, sixteen were purchased between 1961 and 1967. Most had Weymann bodies, and they marked the return to exposed radiators and introduced a new style of destination indicator layout, with the route number relocated to the offside. Seen in Southport on 19 January 1974, number 51 (CWM 151C) was one of the third batch of four buses, and was new in 1965. These were the last Southport buses to have Weymann bodywork, as the final four PD2s were completed by Metro-Cammell in Birmingham.

(John Jones)

Liverpool Corporation introduced motor buses as early as 1911, but they only played a small part of operations for the next twenty years or so, while the tramway system continued to develop and was upgraded right up until 1948. Prior to World War 2 most buses were AECs, but after the war AEC and Leyland took the major orders. The first ten Leyland PD2s appeared in March 1948 and had Leyland bodywork with a further thirty arriving by 1951 which had rare Roberts bodywork, and were Liverpool's last 7 feet 6 inch wide buses. After 1953 the full-width bonnet or tin-front became standard, and between 1954 and 1961, a total of 254 PD2/20 and 49 PD2/30 models were purchased. Here we see L296 (VKB 752), a Leyland PD2/20 with a body shell assembled by Crossley in 1957 and after a period in store completed by Metro-Cammell in late 1961. Bodywork on all 303 buses was complex and featured complete Alexander, Duple, Weymann or Crossley bodies, with others being finished off by Liverpool Corporation or Metro-Cammell, as on L296.

(Chris Aston - Omnicolour)

Liverpool Corporation Transport had a large fleet of AEC Regent III double-deckers delivered between 1948 and 1955. The final examples had full-width bonnets to Liverpool's own design, and they were of the 9613S variant which indicates that they are 27 feet long with a 9.6 litre engine, vacuum-assisted brakes and a synchromesh gearbox. The first example of what was to be a fleet of 192 AEC Regent V double-deckers arrived in 1955 as A101. These were D3RV models and bodywork on the early vehicles was by Crossley, with some buses being finished off in the Corporation's own body shop at Edge Lane works. A106 (SKB 106), with a complete Crossley body, entered service in November 1955. It is seen in the tranquil setting of Menlove Avenue in June 1967 whilst working service 5 to Castle Street. The bodywork carried by later Regent Vs A168 to A292 was based on the Metro-Cammell Orion style, with about thirty examples also being completed in-house by Liverpool Corporation.

(Martin Llewellyn - Omnicolour)

In 1958/59 Liverpool Corporation obtained three double-deckers for evaluation, before making a decision on future orders. They comprised a forward entrance AEC Regent V, an AEC Bridgemaster and a Leyland Atlantean, all of radically different designs. It was the Atlantean that won the day, and an order for two hundred was duly placed for delivery from late 1962 onwards. Numbered L500 to 699, they had 77-seat bodies by Metro-Cammell, with distinctive styling to Liverpool's own requirements. Notable features are the peaked roof domes and ribbed aluminium skirt panels. Liverpool's Pier Head is the setting for this study of L580 in May 1967. The choice of the Atlantean would signal the start of many orders for this type of bus. Merseyside PTE was formed on 1 December 1969, and took under its wing the municipal fleets of Birkenhead and Wallasey to the south of the Mersey, and the extensive Liverpool fleet which at this time stood at around 1100 buses.

(Cliff Essex)

Warrington's early claim to fame was in ancient times when it was regarded as an important crossing place on the River Mersey. It later developed as a major hub on the transport network in the north-west of England, and as a centre for heavy industry, and latterly chemicals. Double-deck petrol-electric buses first appeared in 1913, and when Warrington's trams ended in 1935 two dozen new double-deckers were purchased, comprising six Crossleys and eighteen Leyland Titans. Warrington's early post-war vehicle policy was varied and interesting to say the least. It bought fifteen rare Foden double-deckers prior to 1956, and also successfully operated a number of batches of Leyland Titan PD2s. The purchase of twenty-nine Bristol K6G chassis between 1947 and 1950 was made even more interesting by the choice of bodywork, completed by Welsh coachbuilders Bruce Coachworks, for all but two of these. This attractive view of a Bruce example was taken in Warrington town centre in October 1961. Number 52 (FED 747) was new in 1949, and was taken out of service in 1964.

(Martin Llewellyn - Omnicolour)

The town of Widnes can be found on the northern bank of the River Mersey, and from the mid-nineteenth century onwards rapidly became the centre of a newly developing chemical industry. The Corporation did not run a tramway, and its first venture into public transport operation was in 1909 with four 34-seat double-deck Commer motor buses which were believed to be the first covered-top double-deckers in the country. On the opposite bank of the Mersey to Widnes stands the town of Runcorn which was reached by a railway bridge, and a superb transporter bridge opened in 1905. At around one thousand feet in length, this was the largest of its type in the world. Sadly, it was replaced in 1961, but by an elegant road bridge of single-arch span design. From 1948 the Leyland PD2 became the standard new double-decker, and on a sunny day in June 1962, number 32 (237 WTD) is seen crossing the new bridge on a journey to Runcorn. The bus was one of two delivered in November 1961, and a total of eighteen similar buses were purchased between 1957 and 1966. In post-war years the fleet strength was usually around forty vehicles.

(Martin Llewellyn - Omnicolour)

Barrow-in-Furness is located on the northern edge of Morecambe Bay and is an industrial town and port. It had a very significant shipbuilding industry which is still important in 2010. Barrow-in-Furness Corporation ran its first motor buses in 1923, and while bus operations continued to expand, the existing tramway system finally closed in 1932. Guy and Daimler utility double-deckers were obtained during the war and a major fleet renewal occurred in the early post-war years. This was to include twenty Crossley DD42s and fifty Leyland PD2s with Park Royal bodies. All the PD2s were 8 feet wide and 26 feet long. A further ten arrived in 1958, but this time they were built as 27 feet PD2/40 models. It is one of this later batch, number 166 (CEO 953), that we see in the centre of Barrow in July 1973. Its Park Royal body provided seating for 61 passengers. This vehicle saw service with Barrow until 1977, and after a brief spell as a non-PSV, was still languishing in a scrap yard three years later.

(Andrew Wiltshire collection)

Morecambe and Heysham were neighbouring towns situated on Morecambe Bay. From 1932 until 1960, only AEC buses were purchased by Morecambe and Heysham Corporation, and all those bought in the 1930s were petrol-engined. A large number of AEC Regents was purchased from 1947 onwards and most featured Park Royal bodywork. Of these, thirty-four were Regent III models, of which the 1951 batch of six had attractive bodywork by Weymann. Here we see one of these, number 73 (MTE 635), picking up a group of passengers on the seafront at Morecambe. This bus later passed to Lancaster City Council and was withdrawn in late 1975. Going on to become a driver training and towing vehicle, it was later saved for preservation.

(Peter G Smith - Omnicolor)

The AEC monopoly was broken in 1960 when the first of five Massey-bodied Leyland PD2s arrived; these were to be the only Leylands ever received in fifty-five years of operation. Seen in June 1971 at the depot in Heysham Road, number 89 (35 MTD) was one of three PD2/37 models. They had air brakes and the traditional Leyland exposed radiator. The final two Leylands, 90/91 (435/436 XTF), were delivered in 1962 and featured the St Helens type glass-fibre bonnet. Also clearly visible in this view is the sliding door. Number 89 was later fitted with a separate route number box in March 1972, and after sixteen years service, latterly with Lancaster City Council, was withdrawn in 1976. It ended its days in Scotland, working for Paterson and Brown of Dalry, Ayrshire.

(Cliff Essex collection)

Unlike many smaller Lancashire municipals which remained loyal to Leyland, Lancaster was also keen on Daimlers, taking eighteen COG5 chassis between 1936 and 1940, ten of which were bodied as saloons. In 1937 the title of the undertaking became Lancaster City Transport to reflect Lancaster being granted city status. The post-war years until 1953 saw a mixture of Leyland Tigers and Titans, Crossleys and some Daimler CVG5 saloons. The first of half a dozen forward entrance double-deckers arrived in 1963 numbered 201 to 203. They were Leyland PD2/37 models with seating for 65 in East Lancs bodies, and the final trio would be delivered in 1965. This study of 202 (202 YTE) in Lancaster bus station was taken on 16 July 1975. The first three were converted to open-top in 1976, and 202 had been withdrawn by 1980. This particular bus survives in 2010 with East Yorkshire M.S. as an open-top publicity vehicle.

(John Jones)

Blackpool is probably best known as a very popular northern seaside resort, and to transport enthusiasts its main attraction is likely to be its trams. Bus operation began in 1921, and by 1926 there were as many as thirty-eight motor buses in use. Blackpool continued to expand the tram network during the 1930s and introduced new streamlined tramcars. The bus fleet was not overlooked either, and a series of eighty-eight streamlined Burlingham-bodied Leyland Titans, with centre entrances and seating just 48, entered service between 1936 and 1940. These were gradually replaced in the late 1940s and early 1950s by one hundred equally impressive Leyland Titan PD2/5s, again with a streamlined profile and bodied locally by Burlingham. Here we see 238 (DFV 138) at Gynn Square in September 1963. Blackpool's famous streamlined Leyland PD2s served the town from 1949 until 1969.

(Cliff Essex collection)

Leylands continued to reign supreme at Blackpool during the 1950s, and 1962 would see the arrival of the first 30 feet buses. Numbered 351 to 370, they were ordered as tramway replacements for the inland Marton area routes that had been discontinued. These full-fronted Metro-Cammell-bodied Leyland PD3s would be at a glance, visually very similar to the shorter 27 feet PD2s (306 to 350). They would of course have extra seating, for 73 passengers in this case, and operated as 70-seaters during the summer season. Number 356 (YFR 356) is seen disembarking passengers in Talbot Square in September 1963, with sister bus 353 behind. Both are working service 12 that ran from Talbot Road bus station to Squires Gate. It is pleasing to record that a vehicle from Blackpool's first batch of PD3 chassis, number 351, has been saved for preservation.

(Geoff Gould / copyright Claire Pendrous)

Located on the Fylde coast, Lytham St Annes Corporation served the neighbouring towns of Lytham, and to the west, St Annes. The first post-war double-deckers delivered in 1946 were six very attractive Leyland-bodied PD1 models. These buses had relatively long lives, one example lasting until 1972. The first Leyland PD2s arrived in 1948, again bodied by Leyland and 1951 was to see a further five, but this time to the now increasingly popular width of 8 feet. These buses would be the last vehicles in the fleet with traditional exposed radiators, and the last with Leyland bodies. In 1957, five PD2/20 models with full-width tin-fronts entered service. One of this batch, number 59 (758 CTD), is seen heading along Squires Gate Lane on 8 September 1973. The four-bay bodywork is by Northern Counties of Wigan, a manufacturer new to this fleet with this batch, but one which would feature regularly from 1969. Number 59 passed to Fylde Borough Transport in April 1974, and saw a further fifteen months service.

(John Jones)

Preston was originally a market town that had become industrialised by the mid-nineteenth century. Located on the north bank of the River Ribble, the town also had a small port. At Preston, Leylands were to be the exclusive choice, being manufactured only six miles away. The first double-deckers arrived in 1926 and Leyland Titans formed the bulk of new vehicle purchases throughout the 1930s. The first peace time arrivals were three Leyland-bodied and seven Alexander-bodied (to Leyland design) PD1 models in 1946, to be followed by twenty-one PD1As, six of which had rare Samlesbury bodywork. A pair of East Lancs-bodied Tiger PS1/1 saloons were placed in service in 1949. The chassis had been stored since 1946, and when bodied these buses were 35-seaters, being reduced to 34 at a later date. Number 74 (CRN 79), seen here in Preston in March 1967, was to survive until December 1968, before being sold for use as a mobile polling booth.

(Chris Aston - Omnicolour)

The five Leyland PD3As delivered in 1965 were Preston's last new half-cabs and also the last buses delivered in the maroon and cream livery. The following year a series of livery experiments took place with four PD2s appearing in various blue with either ivory or cream colour schemes. Crossley-bodied number 33 (KRN 424) carries this version of mid blue and ivory which was not deemed a success. It is seen in the depot yard at Deepdale Road. The bus dates from 1957 and was one of thirteen similar buses delivered that year. Similar bus 35 received the version of blue and ivory that was adopted, as seen on PD2 number 48 on the rear cover of this book. 33 was withdrawn in 1974, but the maroon and cream colour scheme had completely disappeared by June 1971.

(Cliff Essex collection)

Blackburn was a boom-town during the Industrial Revolution thanks to textile manufacturing, the history of which can be traced back to the thirteenth century. The first motor buses, six Leyland Tiger TS2s, were introduced in 1929, and throughout the 1930s Leylands continued to be favoured, although two AEC Regents arrived in 1939. During World War 2, Guy Arab utility buses were delivered to Blackburn, and after the war, ten Leyland PS1 saloons, twenty-six PD1 and thirty-five PD1A double-deckers appeared before a move was made to Guy Motors. In 1949 twenty Arab III models with Crossley 56-seat bodies arrived and gave very good service. Number 131 (CBV 431), seen here at Blackburn's Intack garage, suffered serious damage in a low bridge accident in 1969, and after repair it re-entered service with the roof from withdrawn 128. The bus continued in service until 1973, and fortunately for all, is now preserved by the Darwen Transport Museum Trust.

(Andrew Wiltshire collection)

For delivery to Blackburn in 1957, ten new Guy chassis were ordered with eight more to follow in 1958. These were Arab IV models, and they would have locally built 58-seat East Lancs bodywork to 7 feet 6 inch width, featuring new-look bonnets and Gardner 6LW engines. Numbered 140 to 157, the 1957 buses took registration marks HCB 140-149, while KBV 150-157 formed the second delivery. Eight-feet wide buses would not appear with this undertaking until 1961. Here we see 154 on 16 July 1975 in the centre of Blackburn, passing the offices of the Evening Telegraph, and carrying the modified livery that was introduced in 1967. Also of note is that the bus now has a modified front radiator grille, acquired most probably due to accident damage. This particular vehicle was withdrawn in 1976, with the last of the batch, number 152 surviving until 1979 as a training bus.

(John Jones)

The town of Darwen, like Blackburn just over four miles to the north, was an important centre for textile manufacture in the nineteenth century and was one of the first towns in the UK to have steam trams. Motor buses had been plying the streets of Darwen since 1926, and the first double-deckers were Burlingham-bodied Leyland TD5s which arrived in 1937/38. In the early post-war years, Darwen took half a dozen Alexander-bodied PD1 models, while the first of many Leyland PD2s to grace the streets of this Lancashire town were four delivered in 1952. In 1964 the first 30 feet double-deckers made their appearance, and the bus seen here, number 28 (FTD 250B), was one of a pair of the Leyland PD3A/1 type, which also introduced front entrance double-deck bodywork and the St. Helens type bonnet to the fleet. Three more appeared in 1965, after which Darwen reverted to the shorter PD2A/27 model for a further dozen buses. In this view number 28 is seen heading into Darwen along Duckworth Street on a dismal, but atmospheric 21 April 1973. This bus was eventually exported to Budapest in Hungary in 1992, for use as a mobile bar.

(John Jones)

Accrington Corporation Transport began motor bus operation on 12 November 1928 with a service running between Huncoat and Higher Antley and passing through the town centre. Six Dennis saloons were used, and a month later a second service between Accrington and Rawtenstall commenced, run jointly with both Haslingden and Rawtenstall Corporations. The first post-war double-deckers were Leylands, but five East Lancs-bodied Arab IVs with Gardner 6LW engines arrived in 1953, followed by a further eighteen similar buses between 1954 and 1959. Number 147 (388 FTB) was one of a pair delivered in 1958 and is seen here on the jointly operated Bacup to Accrington route in March 1965. It was the oldest bus to pass to Hyndburn in 1974 and was finally withdrawn in January 1975. During the 1960s, the Accrington fleet strength was usually around fifty-six vehicles.

(Martin Llewellyn - Omnicolour)

Accrington received a number of Leyland Titans in the 1930s, and deliveries resumed after the war with both PD1 and PD2 models, and, as explained above, numerous Guy Arabs. Representing the final pair of PD2s is PD2/31, number 154 (949 RTB), parked alongside the depot in Ellison Street. Dating from November 1960, this bus was a 7 feet 6 inch wide model complete with full-width tin-front bonnet, which proudly boasts a splendid Leyland motif, and it can be seen that the lining has now been discontinued from the livery. Number 154 has an East Lancs body similar to that on Guy Arab 147, and with seating for 63 passengers. All future buses for Accrington, commencing with the two Guy Wulfrunians 156 and 157, would be 8 feet wide. Both 154 and sister bus 155 passed to Hyndburn Borough Transport in 1974 (see page 61), and had departed for scrap by 1976.

(Andrew Wiltshire collection)

The Burnley, Colne and Nelson Joint Transport Committee was formed in 1933 by the amalgamation of the existing tram and bus operating municipal fleets in these three towns. Seventy-four new Leyland Titan double-deckers arrived between 1934 and 1935 as tram replacements, and a mixture of Leyland Lion and AEC Regal saloons replaced some of the older inherited motor buses in 1936. The Leyland PD2 first appeared in 1947 and 195 (ACW 560) was one of eight delivered in 1949 with East Lancs bodywork. The next double-deckers delivered were from Guy Motors, sixteen Arab III models after which orders returned to Leyland. Number 195 is seen July 1967 and heading along Church Street in Burnley. It was withdrawn in 1969 and sold for scrap.

(Martin Llewellyn - Omnicolour)

Burnley, Colne and Nelson had depots in Burnley and Colne, and from the 1950s the livery was officially described as madder and cream. Apart from Guy and Daimler utilities during the war, Leyland Titans remained very popular with fifty-four arriving between 1946 and 1950, and early post-war saloons consisted of Leyland Tiger PS1 and PS2 models. In 1959 Burnley, Colne and Nelson took a pair of Leyland PD3s with forward entrances, the first of six such buses with East Lancs 73-seat bodies. Number 236 (LHG 536) was an example new in 1961 and is seen in Burnley bus station in April 1969. All six PD3s passed to Burnley and Pendle in 1974, but were all rapidly sold within a few months to Lancaster City Council, where LHG 536 put in four years service.

(Cliff Essex)

Haslingden Corporation Transport Department operated a small fleet in the Rossendale Valley area of East Lancashire, Haslingden being to the west of Rawtenstall and to the north of Ramsbottom. Apart from weaving, Haslingden was famous for the quarrying of quartz-based sandstone, known as Haslingden Flag and commonly used for paving across the United Kingdom. Trams in the town were operated by Accrington Corporation, and these ceased to run in 1930. At this point Haslingden Corporation commenced joint motor bus operation with Accrington and Rawtenstall Corporations over the former tram route from Accrington to Bacup.

After the wartime utility buses, only vehicles of Leyland manufacture were operated, right up until 1968. Double-deckers first appeared in 1932, and Haslingden Corporation number 11 (PTF 208) was a 1953 Leyland PD2/12 with a 56-seat Leyland body. It is seen in Rawtenstall in March 1965, and was one of three similar vehicles numbered 9 to 11. This bus passed to Rossendale Joint Transport in April 1968 as its number 14 and was withdrawn in 1973, subsequently being sold to a Barnsley breaker.

(Martin Llewellyn - Omnicolour)

The town of Rawtenstall is situated on the banks of the River Irwell and was another settlement famous for its cotton mills. Many fine historical buildings survive in Rawtenstall to this day as a legacy to the textile industry. Leyland was to be the main supplier of buses to Rawtenstall Corporation, and many Leyland PD2s appeared from 1948. The last six were purchased in 1955, and were the only buses in the Rawtenstall fleet with full-width tin fronts. No further double-deckers were purchased until 1964, when some splendid Leyland PD3s arrived. They had East Lancs forward entrance bodies and marked a return to traditional exposed radiators. The first of what was to be a total of twelve was number 30 (FTE 630B). It is seen when almost new at Rawtenstall in August 1964.

(Cliff Essex collection)

The first municipal fleets in Lancashire to disappear in the post-war period were those of Haslingden and Rawtenstall Corporations, when the two fleets amalgamated in 1968. In 1955 Rawtenstall purchased a single Weymann-bodied Leyland Tiger Cub saloon, which had previously been on loan from Leyland Motors, and this was followed by two further East Lancs-bodied examples in 1958 and 1960 (see page 66). In 1964 a pair of attractive 30 feet Leyland Leopards with manual gearboxes and East Lancs 44-seat bodies were delivered. These saloons were used for one-man operation from new, and one of the pair, number 50 (FTE 650B), is seen in Rawtenstall in March 1965.

(Chris Aston - Omnicolour)

Haslingden and Rawtenstall Corporations operated a joint service with Accrington Corporation, which ran from Bacup to Accrington via Rawtenstall and Haslingden. They both shared the same general manager, who incidentally also presided over Ramsbottom UDC from 1951 until 1967. Then on 1 April 1968 a merger took place between the two to form the Rossendale Joint Transport Committee. A fleet of around fifty-three buses was formed and the Haslingden garage in John Street was closed shortly after. Being by far the smaller of the two fleets, Haslingden's splendid blue and cream livery gave way to a livery based on the crimson and cream colours previously used by Rawtenstall Corporation, but incorporating both coats of arms. Representing the Rossendale Joint Transport Committee fleet is 36 (MTJ 436C), a 1965 Leyland PD3/4. It is seen at the head of a line up of four buses in Haslingden on 25 April 1971.

(Chris Aston - Omnicolour)

Ramsbottom UDC was the smallest municipal undertaking in Lancashire, and when it passed to SELNEC PTE the fleet strength stood at thirteen. The livery was vermilion red and cream and the garage was at Stubbins Lane. From 1951 until 1967 Ramsbottom shared a general manager (L T Merrall), with neighbouring municipal fleets Haslingden and Rawtenstall, after which Mr J Mort took over until the PTE absorbed the fleet in November 1969. Early post-war deliveries included the first double-deckers in the form of six Leyland PD2/1 chassis with Leyland highbridge bodywork in 1947. One of these is 21 (HTF 816), seen here in Rawtenstall when nearly eighteen years old in March 1965. The next new buses purchased by Ramsbottom were three splendid Roe-bodied Leyland Royal Tigers, which arrived in 1950, the first of this type to be placed in service in the United Kingdom as service buses. As for number 21, it ran until May 1969 and eventually passed to SELNEC as a withdrawn vehicle.

(Martin Llewellyn - Omnicolour)

Ramsbottom was one of only two Urban District Councils in England to operate a fleet of buses. A further Leyland PD2 arrived in 1951, after which no further double-deckers were added until 1961 when a PD2/24 arrived. This Leyland was the only bus in the Ramsbottom fleet to sport a tin front style bonnet assembly, and the only double-decker with pneumocyclic transmission. Two further PD2s with St Helens style bonnets arrived in 1962 and 1963 before a switch to 30 feet double-deckers took place in 1965. A grand total of eight Leyland PD3s with 74-seat East Lancs bodywork were ordered, and four of these arrived in 1967. They included number 9 (FTF 703F), seen here in Edenfield in April 1968 when barely five months old. The final six PD3s would have exposed radiators, and the last of the order, number 11 (TTD 386H), was actually delivered in full Ramsbottom livery to SELNEC PTE in 1969. This bus had the honour of being the final new half-cab to enter service in the UK, and the only half-cab delivered new to a PTE.

(Cliff Essex)

1970 to deregulation - just eight fleets survive.

In 1962, eight Leyland PD2/40s with East Lancs bodies became the first 8-feet wide buses in the Warrington fleet. This change had been made in anticipation of the planned widening of Sankey Street, which had up until then dictated the use of 7 feet 6 inch wide vehicles. This scheme was however postponed, and when Warrington was faced with having to replace older buses in 1965, Leyland no longer offered a chassis to this restricted width. However, a special order for a dozen PD2/40 chassis to 7 feet 6 inch width and 28 feet 5 inch length was sanctioned by Leyland. These buses arrived in 1965 as 41 to 52 (BED 722-733C) and were fine looking vehicles with East Lancs forward entrance bodies. They are believed to be the last new double-deckers built to this width, to enter service in the UK. Number 52 is seen in March 1966 passing through the town centre on the Dallam service.

(Martin Llewellyn - Omnicolour)

Warrington was an early customer for Daimler's rear engine Fleetline and received nine examples in 1963. They were numbered 18 to 26 and had East Lancs bodies which seated 77 passengers. Number 23 (5832 ED), new in September 1963, is seen in Horsemarket Street on 24 March 1973. A further similar pair, 27 and 28 arrived in 1965, but these had distinctive curved windscreens and lacked engine shrouds. By 1974 Warrington had twenty-six Fleetlines in service, and number 23 would continue in service until 1981 by which time it had been renumbered 123. The Lancashire town of Warrington became part of the reorganised county of Cheshire on 1 April 1974. The municipal fleet survives to this day having developed its operations to serve many rural areas of Cheshire radiating from Warrington, and still operating from the garage at Wilderspool Causeway opened in 1964.

(John Jones)

No new double-deckers entered the Widnes fleet after 1966, and the single-decker policy went on to specify Leyland Leopards and later Bristol RESLs all with East Lancs bodywork. The Corporation did from time to time purchase second-hand vehicles and in 1955 a quartet of AEC Regent II double-deckers arrived from London Transport's post-war STL class. They were the only AECs ever operated and the six PD2s that came from Wigan in 1969/70, would have fitted into this predominantly Leyland fleet much more easily. The former Wigan buses were Leyland-bodied PD2/12s and a further four Titans arrived in 1972. This time they had equally attractive Massey bodywork with platform doors, and were tin-fronted PD2/30 models, the only Widnes half-cabs that did not have exposed radiators. DJP 751, seen here inside the garage in Moor Lane, was new in 1958 as Wigan number 7, and in Widnes became number 16. It was withdrawn in 1976 and sold for scrap. By that time Widnes Corporation had ceased to exist, the town having been incorporated into the county of Cheshire and the undertaking given the new title Halton Borough Transport. Halton also survives as an arms length municipal fleet in 2010 (see page 80).

(Andrew Wiltshire collection)

In 1965 Southport Corporation took a number of buses on loan to conduct trials, with a view to introducing one-man operation. In early 1968, eight forward entrance Leyland PD2s were adapted for use as one-man buses, but by that summer, a dozen far more suitable Leyland Panthers had been delivered. They had smart Metro-Cammell dual-doorway bodywork with seating for 45 passengers and standing capacity of 17, and this view of number 64 (HWM 64F) in Lord Street, Southport, was taken on 19 January 1974. A further ten Panthers, but this time with Marshall bodywork, arrived in September 1971. Southport's last new buses were a batch of ten distinctive looking Alexander-bodied Atlanteans delivered in 1973, followed by eight Leyland Nationals in early 1974. In April 1974 Southport became part of the Metropolitan Borough of Sefton, and its buses passed to the Merseyside PTE.

(John Jones)

St. Helens was one of three Lancashire municipal fleets to be absorbed into the newly-formed Metropolitan counties on 1 April 1974. The residents of this town would see their red and cream buses gradually repainted into Verona green and cream and all local identity would be lost after Merseyside PTE took over operations. The final front engine double-deckers were delivered to St. Helens in 1967 in the form of three AEC Regent V and six Leyland PD2A models. The undertaking then adopted a single-deck policy and no rear engined double-deckers would ever be operated. The AEC Swift chassis was chosen for the introduction of one-man operation, and the two-door bodywork by Marshall had capacity for 20 standees. The first eighteen arrived in 1968 and a further forty-five arrived before the PTE took over operations, at which point nine Swifts were still on order. Number 272 (PDJ 272L) is one of the 1973 batch and is seen in St Helens on 20 April 1973.

(John Jones)

Wigan received its first Leyland PD3s in 1959, which also signified the change to a forward entrance for its double-deckers. The two buses seen here were new in 1961, and are both PD3A/2 models with seating for seventy passengers, and have the St Helens type bonnet. Number 58 (HEK 706) was one of seven with Massey bodywork, whilst making an interesting comparison, particularly with respect to livery application, is number 74 (HJP 9) with a body completed by Northern Counties. Both are seen at the Abram terminus on Warrington Road to the south of the town centre, and will be working across town to Marsh Green. An unusual feature on Wigan's buses was the green light on either side of the destination indicator. These were a legally permissible way of enabling intending passengers to distinguish Wigan buses from those of other operators at night. Wigan Corporation buses did not carry any external advertising and always had a well-cared for appearance.

(A M Davies - Omnicolour)

In 1961, what were to be Barrow's last double-deckers for many years were some Massey-bodied Leyland PD2A/27s with 64 seats. They had a forward entrance layout, complete with a sliding door. Originally numbered 1 to 10, these attractive buses featured St. Helens style fibre-glass bonnets, and became 101 to 110 in 1970 to make way for new deliveries. From 1961 there followed a period when Leyland Leopard saloons were delivered introducing further one-man operation which continued until the end of the decade. In 1974 local government reorganisation saw Barrow cease to be part of Lancashire, and the town was incorporated into the newly-created County of Cumbria, in which it remains today. Number 103 was eventually withdrawn in 1980 and sold for scrap in 1981. Sadly, the municipal fleet at Barrow struggled to survive in the wake of deregulation in 1986, and sold out to Ribble on 26 May 1989. Subsequently, Barrow became part of the Stagecoach group. This view of number 103 (HEO 273) was actually taken after Barrow had become part of Cumbria, but the appearance of the vehicle did not change.

(Cliff Essex)

Lancaster purchased five Leyland Tiger Cubs in the late 1950s, which were then followed in 1961 by three Leyland Leopards that featured centre exits. These eight buses continued the introduction of one-man operation in Lancaster which had commenced in 1957 with some former Rochdale AEC Regal IVs. The next generation of saloons would be of the rear engine variety and also 36 feet in length, thereby offering a greater seating capacity. Six Leyland Panthers were ordered, three for 1967 and three for the following year, and all would have 53-seat East Lancs bodies. Lancaster bus station is the setting for 104 (GTC 104F) on 23 April 1973, and the livery carried at this time was officially known as ruby and broken white. All six Panthers passed to Lancaster City Council in 1974, and GTC 104F saw some further service with a minor Yorkshire operator in 1978, but was sold for scrap in 1979. Lancaster City Transport had become Lancaster City Council Passenger Transport Department in April 1974.

(John Jones)

Morecambe & Heysham Corporation was in fact the larger of the two fleets which combined on 1 April 1974 when the municipal borough of Morecambe and Heysham became part of the District of Lancaster, with Lancaster City Council being the governing body. The six AEC Swifts delivered in 1967 were the first new buses delivered with route-number blinds. They were purchased to introduce one-man operation to the fleet and were numbered 1 to 6. Fitted with Pennine bodies, they had seating for 50 and standing room for 17 passengers. Number 7 arrived in 1968 and was of similar specification, whereas 8 to 10 of 1970 vintage had rather plain Northern Counties bodywork. Here we see Swift number 6 in Morecambe on 23 April 1973. All ten passed to Lancaster City Council in 1974, but their stay would be brief.

(John Jones)

The last new buses for Morecambe & Heysham Corporation were a pair of Seddon RUs, delivered in September 1973. Taking fleet numbers 15 and 16, they brought the number of this type of bus in the fleet to six. The pair were to dual-purpose specification, seating 47, and wore a curious but not unattractive livery of Heysham green and Chelsea blue. They passed to Lancaster City Council a few months later, and in due course received the blue and white livery. 15 (NTF 715M) is seen in Morecambe on the cold morning of 22 January 1977, working a service to Lancaster University. The Seddons proved to be as unreliable as the AEC Swifts before them, and all were sold by January 1978. They found new homes including 15 and 16, which passed to AA Motor Services member, Dodds of Troon in 1978. Their days in Scotland were brief, and both had been scrapped by 1982.

(Geoff Gould / copyright Claire Pendrous)

Amongst the buses inherited from Morecambe & Heysham were two dozen AEC Regent III double-deckers, most of which were well over twenty years of age, and a number were in open-top form. Number 69 (LTF 254), of 1950 vintage and with a Park Royal body, is seen running along Morecambe seafront on 27 August 1974. The livery introduced in 1974 for all vehicles in the newly-created Lancaster City Council fleet was Trafalgar blue and white. However, a number of older, former Morecambe & Heysham buses retained the green and cream livery for a while, but like number 69, they gained the City of Lancaster fleet name. At some stage later in its life, it has had a route number box added, unlike the bus on page 29 which has the route number in its upper deck front window. Number 69 was eventually withdrawn from service in January 1975 and was sold for preservation. The last Regent IIIs, albeit in open-top layout, finally bowed out after the 1979 season.

(Malcolm Keeley)

Upon its formation on 1 April 1974, Lancaster City Council's bus fleet included fifty vehicles inherited from Morecambe and Heysham Corporation. A fleet renewal was urgently needed, and vehicle shortages in 1974 led to the purchase of a number of second-hand buses. From Burnley and Pendle came six Leyland PD3s, which despite their age, were attractive from the point of view of their high seating capacity and forward entrances. They initially entered service in their previous owner's livery, but were soon to gain the new blue and white colour scheme. Some four years later we see 537 (LHG 537) hard at work on a private hire duty in Lancaster on 27 May 1978. All had been withdrawn by July 1978, and this particular bus passed to well-known South Wales independent Llynfi of Maesteg. It was eventually exported to the Netherlands for use as a publicity bus in about 1999. Painted red, it became known as the Double-Decker Diner.

(John Jones)

The AEC Swift, introduced in 1965, received a mixed reception from a number of municipal operators, many of whom were to struggle with reliability problems. Several fleets in north west England adopted this model for their rear engine saloon, and Blackpool persevered with it longer than some other UK fleets. All the Blackpool Swifts were bodied by Marshall and the first examples arrived in 1969/70 numbered 541 to 555. They had seating for 47 passengers and 20 standees, featured dual doors, and all entered service as one-man operated vehicles. The livery must be described as bland, the only relief to the cream being the green painted wheels. Number 577 was new in 1974 and is seen heading along Lytham Road on 3 September 1977, working service 12 and bound for Blackpool Airport at Squires Gate. From 1979 some of the Swifts started to receive a green roof and waistband, and the last examples ran in Blackpool in February 1988.

(John Jones)

The rear engine double-decker was rather late coming to the Blackpool fleet, as the initial programme of one-man conversions had covered routes with traffic levels that were ideal for the AEC Swifts. A survey concluded that the remainder would still require double-deckers, and so after evaluating a number of types, two dozen long-wheelbase East Lancs-bodied Atlanteans were ordered. This was later increased to thirty buses which would arrive as 301 to 330 between 1977 and 1979, and introduced a new livery with a healthy application of green. A further ten arrived in 1980, at which point a small number of the early Swifts were taken out of service, together with further Leyland PD3s. One of the 1980 buses, number 333 (AHG 333V), is seen at Halfway House on 13 September 1986. Blackpool Tower can just be seen in the distance. The Atlantean was a very successful bus at Blackpool and would not be finally phased out until 2009.

(John Jones)

The first municipal-owned rear engine double-deckers on the Fylde coast were a trio delivered to Lytham St. Annes in November 1970. Although ideal for one-man operation, they were however used as crew-operated vehicles until 1975. On 8 September 1973 we see a rather scruffy looking 77 (ATD 281J) heading along Squires Gate Lane near its home depot. These three Northern Counties-bodied Atlanteans went on to serve Fylde for a number of years, as 75 and 76 were withdrawn in 1983, but 77 soldiered on beyond deregulation, passing with the Fylde fleet to Blackpool Transport in 1994. In 1996 it was then preserved by the Lancastrian Transport Trust and now awaits a full restoration. After the formation of Fylde Borough Council, many more new Atlanteans joined the Fylde fleet, but were of the later, improved, AN68 variety.

(John Jones)

In order to accelerate the conversion of services to one-man operation, Fylde Borough Council purchased a small batch of used Leyland Atlanteans in early 1977. Half a dozen thirteen-year old examples came from Merseyside PTE, that had originally been new to Liverpool Corporation. They had Metro-Cammell bodies and were from Liverpool's inaugural batch of 200 Atlanteans, dating from 1963/64 (see page 26). They were allocated fleet numbers 89 to 94, but 91 was only ever used by Fylde as a source of spare parts. The remainder were placed in service between July 1977 and May 1978. The new Fylde livery suited them particularly well as can be judged on 89 (603 KD), seen here in Blackpool in June 1978 as it makes its way to Talbot Road bus station on the route from Lytham via St. Annes. Some of these distinctive double-deckers put in nearly six years service, with number 89 being withdrawn in April 1983.

(John Wiltshire collection)

Following on from six Seddon RUs, the next saloons ordered by Lytham St. Annes were five Bristol RESLs with Leyland engines, ECW bodies and 44 seats. They were to dual-purpose specification but only had four-speed gearboxes. Lytham's order for Bristol REs was eventually delivered to Fylde Borough Council in June 1975 and numbered 37 to 41 with registrations HRN 104-108N. One of these splendid buses, number 38, is seen off service, and leaving Talbot Road bus station in Blackpool on 25 August 1980. Behind the bus are a Blackpool PD3A and an AEC Swift in their rather uninspiring cream livery. Fylde's five Bristol REs would be renumbered 14 to 18 in March 1992, and they would see a very respectable eighteen years service with the fleet. All were withdrawn from service between April and August 1993, with the entire batch passing immediately to the Northern Bus Company of Anston near Sheffield. Sadly, and somewhat surprisingly, none has survived into preservation.

(John Jones)

Preston Corporation was an enthusiastic Titan customer from the model's earliest days, and latterly purchased both PD2 and PD3 models. In 1959, however, it embarked on a very ambitious engineering project using its own workshops. They took a five year-old PD2/10 with a lowbridge open platform Leyland body, and rebuilt it into a 30 feet long highbridge double-decker with a forward entrance, thus in effect creating a 7 feet 6 inch wide PD3. The chassis was extended using parts obtained from Leyland, and a further seven examples followed over the next eight years. In 1963 the fifth conversion created number 50 (SRN 375), seen here on 24 January 1976 on the approach to Preston bus station. Displaying a healthy coating of road grime which is to be expected during January, this bus started out as FRN 734 in 1954 and had a highbridge body, one of the last built by Leyland. It was withdrawn in February 1978 and sold for scrap.

(John Jones)

Preston's iconic bus station was opened in 1969 and, with around eighty stands, was at one time claimed to be the second largest bus station in western Europe. Preston bought its last new half cabs in 1965 and completed its final Leyland PD3 rebuild in 1967. The following year it embraced one-man operation, initially with saloons and later with double-deckers. The first of a large fleet of long-wheelbase Leyland Atlanteans started to arrive in 1975. The initial batch of ten along with a further ten in 1980 had Alexander bodywork, while the remainder were products of the East Lancs factory in neighbouring Blackburn. Alexander-bodied number 146 (UHG 146V) is of 1980 vintage and is seen on the bus station apron, having reversed off its stand, on 14 September 1985. It carried the improved livery with extra ivory that was introduced in late 1973.

(Andrew Wiltshire)

Preston Corporation's first one-man buses were introduced in 1968 and comprised fifteen Leyland Panthers. Five had Metro-Cammell bodies while the remainder were from Marshall of Cambridge. Further Panthers arrived in the years 1970 to 1972, including five with Marshall Camair bodies acquired third-hand, but unused, having been ordered by Stratford Blue. Preston had a requirement for some small buses to be used on a new route serving a pre-war housing estate that was unsuitable for normal size PSVs, so in May 1976 three Bristol LHS6L chassis with very unusual Duple Dominant coach bodies were placed in service. They were 24 feet 10 inches long and 7 feet 6 inches wide and were numbered 242 to 244. The last two had bus seats while 242 had coach-type seats and was occasionally made available for private hire work. They were later renumbered 342 to 344 in 1977 and finally 42 to 44 in 1983. Here we see number 44 (PHG 244P), leaving Preston bus station in August 1984. All three were withdrawn in January 1987.

(Andrew Wiltshire collection)

The AEC Reliance would be the first post-war single-decker type for Darwen, and three with East Lancs 43-seat bodies arrived in 1957/58. They wore a cream livery with red trim and carried Crossley badges, which apparently enabled AEC to secure more space at the Commercial Motor Show. Here we see number 18 (435 BTE), one of the 1957 pair, about to turn into the garage in Fisher Street, wearing a later livery. This bus is obviously very well cared for, and of note is the ornamental trim on both the front and side of the body. Double-deckers dominated the fleet in the 1950s and most of the 1960s, until Darwen Corporation turned to the Bristol RE saloon for all future vehicle requirements. On 1 April 1974 a new municipal borough named Blackburn with Darwen was created and at this point the Darwen fleet was merged with that of Blackburn. The garage in Fisher Street remained in use, and the exchanging of vehicles between here and Blackburn regularly took place. The vehicle in this view was withdrawn in 1973, and therefore did not pass to the new authority.

(Andrew Wiltshire collection)

In 1961 Blackburn took its first 8 feet wide buses, which were to be its last Guys, a dozen Arab IVs with distinctive Johannesburg style bonnets. In 1962 the first of twenty-four Leyland PD2A/24s with pneumocyclic transmission began to arrive, and replaced amongst other buses, the re-bodied war-time Guy Arabs. The second batch of twelve entered service in 1964 and would be Blackburn's last new front engine double-deckers. Again they had East Lancs bodywork with open rear platforms, and some featured fluorescent lighting. The first withdrawals took place in June 1978 and two years later on 24 May 1980 we see number 38 (ABV 38B) passing the railway station in Blackburn. It carries the livery introduced in 1974.

(John Jones)

The Borough of Blackburn Transport introduced a new Brunswick green, cherry red and white livery which, it was felt, reflected the principal colours of the two fleets of Blackburn and Darwen that made up this enlarged municipal fleet from 1 April 1974. The Leyland Atlantean first appeared in the Blackburn fleet in July 1968 as fleet numbers 45 to 54. They had East Lancs bodies and a further eight similar buses arrived in 1971. From 1972 the much improved AN68 version became available, and Blackburn was to receive eighty-nine of these including 123 (CBV 123S), seen here parked in the bus station known as The Boulevard. This bus was one of the

1978 delivery, and was allocated to the Darwen depot when new. With this batch the livery was modified to incorporate a deeper area of green. The Atlantean in the background carries the original version of this livery introduced from 1974. The Boulevard's concrete shelters were built in the 1950s. Those to the south served Ribble routes whilst those to the north served Blackburn. The Whitbread brewery in the background was demolished in 1986 to be replaced by a supermarket. The Dutton family had had a brewery on the site since 1799 and the family-owned company was taken over by Whitbread in 1964.

(Arthur Day collection)

Blackburn's first rear engine saloons were half a dozen unusual East Lancs-bodied Seddon RUs delivered in 1972, and although Blackburn did not buy any Bristol REs from new, it inherited seven with Leyland engines from Darwen Corporation in 1974. In 1978 the undertaking experienced a vehicle shortage, and hired some Leyland PD3As from Leicester City Transport, which were followed by the purchase of five ECW-bodied Bristol RESLs in October 1978 from the same fleet. These buses, LJF 1-5F, dated from late 1967 and had 41-seat dual-door bodywork, a first for the Blackburn fleet, though the centre doors were not used. They entered service from the Darwen depot, and it is in Darwen that we see number 152 (LJF 2F) on 5 September 1980. In the background can be seen Darwen Tower on Beacon Hill, a monument erected in 1898 to celebrate Queen Victoria's Diamond Jubilee. Bristol RE number 152 was to have a brief stay in the Blackburn fleet, being sold in early 1981.

(Malcolm Keeley)

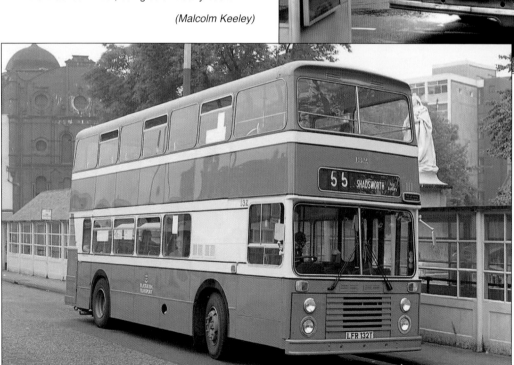

Despite standardising on the Leyland Atlantean chassis for over ten years, in 1979 Blackburn decided to order a pair of the new Dennis Dominator double-deck chassis. Upon delivery, the two buses, bodied by East Lancs of course, were numbered 131 and 132 and registered LFR 131/132T. In 1983 another new livery based on the pre-war olive green and ivory scheme appeared, but used a lighter shade of green known as county green. This was then adopted and is seen here on Dominator number 132. The location is Blackburn's Boulevard on 26 July 1983 and the bus is serving the Shadsworth housing estate. In the background to the left is the Palace theatre built in 1899 and later converted to a cinema and finally a bingo hall before eventual demolition in late 1988. Blackburn returned to Atlanteans once more in 1980/81, but did buy a further five Dominators in 1981, which were numbered 1 to 5 starting a new numbering series. Upon deregulation in 1986, both 131 and 132 were loaned to Rennies of Dunfermline, and later sold to them. The five later Dominators did not really fare any better, being taken out of service in June 1987 and sold to Warrington Borough Transport, ending their days with Chester City Transport.

(Andrew Wiltshire)

Accrington Corporation Transport was destined to become Hyndburn Borough Transport in 1974. The name Hyndburn is that of a local river that passes through Haslingden and Accrington before joining the River Calder. After adding three unusual Guy Arab LUF saloons to its fleet in 1956, Accrington turned in 1962 to the Leyland Tiger Cub for its single-deck requirements. A total of eight Tiger Cubs with East Lancs 43-seat bodies would be obtained, numerically the last of them being 24 (RTD 506C), new in 1965. This was a PSUC1/13 type which tells us that it has a pneumocyclic gearbox, making lighter work for its drivers. On 16 July 1975 in Accrington, we see number 24, which is now working for Hyndburn Borough Transport, and is running on service 8 to neighbouring Oswaldtwistle. The last Tiger Cubs ran for Hyndburn in 1978, and number 24 was to find a new life as a glider winch with the British Aerospace Gliding Club at Woodford, Cheshire.

(John Jones)

Accrington purchased its first Leyland Atlanteans in 1969, and took a dozen new examples before the fleet was restyled Hyndburn Borough Transport in 1974. This example, 177 (HTF 177K) was new in 1971, and part of a batch of four. Although retaining the same basic colours as Accrington Corporation, Hyndburn modernised the livery using an extra lower red band, with the second band stepping up at the front of the bus. The morning of 14 September 1985 was a little damp in Rawtenstall, but the photographer was cheered up with the arrival of 177, on its way to Bacup, which was still a joint service with Rossendale. Hyndburn's loyalty to the Atlantean appeared to come to an end in 1978, after which Dennis Dominators found favour. However, many second-hand Atlanteans were purchased after deregulation.

(Andrew Wiltshire)

Hyndburn did not receive its first Leyland Leopards until 1977, marking a swing away from the rear engine Bristol RESL. In 1981 Dennis Specialist Vehicles introduced the Falcon H chassis, which in some ways offered customers a replacement for the much-loved Bristol RE. The Falcon featured a Gardner 6HLX engine and a Voith gearbox, and Hyndburn was to order two for delivery from East Lancs with dual-purpose seating. Number 50 would arrive in April 1984, while 51 (B51 XFV) entered service ten months later. Despite this model having some reliability issues, the Hyndburn pair continued to run following the demise of that fleet. After a few subsequent owners in the north west, number 51 was eventually exported to Malta by 2002, where it is still in service in 2010. In this view 51 was only seven months old, when noted in Accrington bus station on 14 September 1985.

(Andrew Wiltshire)

At Burnley, Colne and Nelson the rear-engine saloon fleet offered the enthusiast considerable variety. After a batch of ten Leyland Panthers, Burnley, Colne and Nelson took twenty Bristol RESL single-deckers with Leyland engines, followed in 1972 by a similar number of Gardner-powered Seddon RU saloons with Pennine bodywork. These were numbered 111 to 130 and the last five were completed as dual-purpose vehicles. The final Burnley, Colne and Nelson buses were five 44-seat Leyland Nationals in 1973. Burnley bus station on 21 April 1973 was the setting for this view of number 127 (SHG 127K), one of the final batch of ten Seddons. The Seddon RU had design flaws which were never rectified, and many of Burnley's examples had short lives, being withdrawn between 1979 and 1982.

(John Jones)

Burnley, Colne and Nelson reverted to shorter Leyland PD2As in 1962 after trying half a dozen 30 feet Titans that were numbered 233 to 238 (see page 37). The subject of this view, number 239 (NHG 539), was one of the original batch of four PD2As from 1962, and is laying over in Burnley bus station on a rather dismal 10 June 1977, with a Ribble PD3 driver-trainer emerging from the depot in the background. The PD2As were to be the last double-deck buses purchased by the Burnley, Colne and Nelson undertaking, with all twenty-six passing to Burnley and Pendle in 1974. Not being readily suitable for conversion to one-man operation, withdrawals of this type began in 1976 following the arrival of several new Bristol VRT double-deckers. At first, the 1964 batch and five of the 1965 examples were sold, most finding ready buyers among independent operators. The final half-cabs in service with Burnley and Pendle (260 to 263) were withdrawn early in 1980, with 262 being retained as a training bus for a few extra months.

(John Jones)

On 1 April 1974 the towns of Colne and Nelson were merged into a new district to be known as Pendle. Consequently, the Burnley, Colne and Nelson Joint Transport Committee became Burnley and Pendle Joint Transport. As mentioned on page 63, twenty Bristol RESL chassis were purchased by Burnley, Colne and Nelson in the years 1970/71. The first five had Northern Counties bodywork, a fairly rare combination, while the next five had East Lancs bodywork which was not uncommon amongst Lancashire municipalities. However, the last ten were to receive Pennine bodywork, though this was not the original plan. Due to long delays caused by a serious fire at the East Lancs factory at Easter 1970, the order was transferred to the Oldham-based firm. The body has a strong likeness to the Seddon RUs that followed in 1972 (see page 63), with the front mounted radiator grille being the most obvious distinguishing feature. After passing to Burnley and Pendle in 1974, all would see a further eight to nine years service before sale. Pictured here close to Burnley bus station on 25 September 1981 is number 106 (PHG 806K).

(John Jones)

The Rossendale Joint Transport Committee ceased to exist in 1974 when local government reorganisation saw the formation of Rossendale Borough Council. By late 1976 the fleet stood at sixty-two vehicles, of which only sixteen were double-deckers, all Leyland Titans. Saloons inherited in 1968 from Rawtenstall Corporation included a pair of Leyland Tiger PS2s, a Royal Tiger, three Tiger Cubs and a pair of Leopards. Two of the Tiger Cubs, 58 and 59, were particularly interesting being PSUC1/5 versions with constant mesh gearboxes and only 7 feet 6 inches wide. They had attractive 44-seat East Lancs bodies, and here we see number 58 (466 FTJ) working for Rossendale Borough Council in Rawtenstall on 10 June 1977. It is pleasing to record that after withdrawal in 1979, number 58 passed into preservation, and in 2010 is still active on the rally scene.

(John Jones)

The formation of the Rossendale fleet in 1968 saw vehicle policy concentrate on reliable and rugged Leyland Leopard saloons. However, in 1974 when the Borough Council took over from the Joint Transport Committee, the first new buses were five Bristol RESLs with East Lancs bodies. Rossendale was thus a late convert to rear engine buses, the RESL having first appeared with north-west municipal fleets in 1968. Number 9 (YTC 309N) is seen on a wet 14 September 1985 waiting at the bus stands in Bacup Road, Rawtenstall. The building behind, clad in scaffolding, is part of Rossendale's garage. Four more similar RESLs were bought in 1975, and all survived with Rossendale after deregulation. Some lasted until at least 1991, with several going for further service.

(Andrew Wiltshire)

Rossendale was also a late convert to the rear engine double-decker, having expanded one-man operation using saloons for a good number of years. The type eventually chosen would be the East Lancs-bodied Atlantean, a truly Lancashire vehicle. Deliveries commenced in 1977 with three AN68A type chassis and 75-seat bodies, and introduced a livery featuring more cream. The vehicle in this view is number 25 (DDK 25W), dating from 1980, and is seen arriving in Burnley on a pleasant 25 August 1981. Eventually a total of fourteen Atlanteans were purchased new by Rossendale, but the Atlantean story would not end there, as numerous examples were later acquired from other operators. The final new buses acquired prior to deregulation were a pair of Bristol LHs with rather angular East Lancs 28-seat bodies. These were needed for the service from Rawtenstall to Cowpe, where there was a length restriction when turning the bus without the aid of a conductor.

(John Jones)

Deregulation and beyond.

Under the Conservative government of Margaret Thatcher, the Transport Act of 1985 paved the way for the deregulation of local bus services throughout the whole of the United Kingdom except London. This would eventually have far reaching consequences for most bus operators throughout the county. Privatisation and competition were now all the rage, and too many long established fleets that we thought would be with us forever, simply disappeared without trace. Shortly before

Deregulation Day on 26 October 1986, we see Blackpool Transport Leyland PD3A number 507 (HFR 507E) busy at work on 13 September, during the early part of the Blackpool Illuminations. This is a time when the transport system in this seaside town is pushed to the very limit. Blackpool's Leyland half-cabs enjoyed extended lives compared to those in other municipal fleets, and did not finally bow out until November 1988. The PD3 is wearing the later livery that featured a much healthier application of green.

(John Jones)

Blackpool Transport was faced with a number of issues when it became an arms-length operation upon deregulation. The fleet still had a number of AEC Swifts in service, and to replace these around fifteen second-hand Leyland Nationals were purchased between 1986 and 1987. Four were sourced from Crosville, and were long-wheelbase examples such as number 145 (CFM 345S). It is seen on 18 September 1988, about to turn out of Tyldesley Road on its way to Victoria Hospital. This bus carries a Blackpool Transport fleet name, and nearly two years after deregulation there is no trace of a coat of arms. A prominent Gardner badge indicates that 145 has lost its original Leyland 510 engine in favour of a 6HLX unit. The four Leyland Nationals supplied by Crosville were in fact converted to Gardner power for Blackpool Transport, using engines recovered from Crosville's once numerous Seddon RU fleet.

(John Wiltshire)

Burnley and Pendle purchased two batches of Bristol VRTs in the 1970s to replace the last Leyland Titans in the fleet, and complete the conversion of services to one-man operation. The first fourteen vehicles arrived in 1976 and had distinctive East Lancs bodywork, and in 1978 a further ten entered service but with 74-seat ECW bodies. An opportunity arose in 1982 to purchase some five year old, long-wheelbase VRTs from Tayside Regional Transport, and eventually six were obtained. They had Alexander bodies which were then converted to single-door layout for use in Burnley. Meanwhile one of the ECW variety, number 173 (FFR 173S), still looked good on 13 August 1990 at twelve years of age. The livery is a later style introduced after deregulation and the fleet title features the Pendle Witch logo. The Bristol VRTs have long gone from the area and 173 was to be scrapped, but sister bus 174 is still thought to survive in the United States, most probably in use as a sightseeing bus.

(John Jones)

By the second half of 1987 the financial fortunes of Burnley and Pendle allowed some new vehicles to be ordered. In a complete break with tradition Volvo was chosen to supply underfloor engine chassis which would comprise two Citybus coach-seated double-deckers, and six Volvo B10M dual purpose saloons. For delivery in early 1988, Alexander would supply R type bodies for the double-deckers which became fleet numbers 101 and 102, while the saloons became numbers 61 to 66 and had P-type bodies seating 53. Further examples were later added to the fleet up until 1993. One of the original Citybuses, number 101 is seen in Burnley on 28 September 1988, after a heavy shower. The revised livery is caught to good effect and the high-backed coach-type seats are very obvious in this view.

(John Jones)

Burnley and Pendle purchased five former London Buses AEC Routemasters in 1988 principally for use on the "main line" service from Burnley to Colne via Nelson, and also for the Burnley to Nelson via Marsden Cross service. These were launched under the brand East Enders and were intended to fend off competition on these corridors. Each bus was given a mainly red livery and an appropriate name taken from the East Enders TV series, and ran successfully for two years. Number 180 is seen here in September 1988, and displays the name Queen Vic after the famous pub in the soap opera. Following its acquisition of Ribble, Stagecoach became very active in the Burnley area, and in 1996 Pendle Council put its share of the Burnley and Pendle fleet up for sale. Despite a number of bidders, the sale to Stagecoach was then completed, and after dragging its heels Burnley Council also succumbed, and sold its share to Stagecoach.

(John Jones)

By 1983 Lancaster's fortunes had dramatically improved. The conversion to one-man operation was complete and the introduction of more modern and reliable buses had enabled elderly and troublesome types to be sold off. The first new double-deckers to be purchased for many years arrived in 1979 in the form of three 78-seat East Lancs-bodied Atlanteans. Many more would follow. One example is number 206 (LFV 206X), seen here in June 1993 wearing the final livery style. Following a period of intense competition between 1986 and 1989, Lancaster City Transport Ltd responded and increased service frequencies which meant adding quite a few used vehicles to stock. In December 1992 the bus operation was placed on the market by Lancaster City Council with interest being expressed by MTL Merseybus and Blackpool Transport. However, on 22 August 1993 after further intense competition from Stagecoach, the business was wound up, with some dozen or so buses and the garage being sold to Stagecoach North West for just over £1 million.

(Andrew Wiltshire collection)

Blackburn Borough Transport Ltd was the title of the new council-owned company that came into being at deregulation. At this time only two former Darwen buses were still in service, both Bristol RESLs, and the former Darwen garage had already closed in 1982. The year 1987 saw the arrival of the first of many second-hand buses in the form of Alexander-bodied Leopards from Scotland. Then, to replace double-deckers, Leopard and Tiger coaches were acquired, as well as a number of former Ribble Bristol RESLs. Local coachbuilder East Lancs launched the Leyland National Greenway in 1991 which was basically a heavily re-engineered National with many new or refurbished components. Blackburn Transport took twenty-three examples between 1993 and 1995. Here we see number 427 (LRN 552N) in Blackburn in July 1993. The bus began life as South Yorkshire PTE's JDT 437N, and entered service in its rebuilt form with Blackburn in 1993. New buses were also acquired and between 1991 and 1999, many Volvo saloons arrived.

(Andrew Wiltshire collection)

By 1999 the remaining Atlanteans, mainly used on schools and contract work, were in desperate need of replacement. To facilitate this, as only limited funds were available, a decision was made to acquire second-hand double-deckers. These initially took the form of Leyland Olympians from London and Lothian but were later joined by eleven Leyland Titans also from London. Many of these ended up on front line work like number 96 (KYV 526X) seen here arriving at Blackburn's Boulevard in June 2002. This bus, which dated from 1982, had entered service the previous month. The first new double-deckers for nearly twenty years, five Dennis Tridents with 90 seats arrived in 2002, and introduced another new livery incorporating yellow bands. On 16 August 2006 a decision was made by Blackburn with Darwen Council to sell Blackburn Borough Transport Ltd to Blazefield Holdings. The end came on 21 January 2007 when the fleet became part of Blazefield's Lancashire United operation.

(Andrew Wiltshire collection)

In the three years running up to deregulation new buses delivered to Fylde had comprised Northern Counties-bodied Leyland Atlanteans and a solitary Duple Dominant bus-bodied Leyland Tiger. In 1985 the first five of nearly thirty second-hand Roe-bodied Atlanteans arrived from Kingston-upon-Hull Transport. Number 46 (TKH 276H) was new in 1969 and is seen on Lytham Road in Blackpool on 17 October 1987, still in its previous owner's livery. Also worthy of mention are a trio of double-deckers from Grimsby-Cleethorpes Transport with Roe bodies similar to the former Hull buses, which would be the only Daimler Fleetlines to be owned. By 1987 Fylde Borough Transport Ltd had adopted the name Blue Buses and was experiencing serious competition from Blackpool, and what had originally been a fleet of around thirty-two vehicles had risen to ninety-eight by 1989.

(Andrew Wiltshire)

Particularly interesting acquisitions by Fylde were four Atlantean chassis acquired in 1992 from Kingston-upon-Hull. They had been new to the Bradford municipal undertaking and their bodies had been scrapped by a Barnsley breaker. The chassis were refurbished and modified by Fylde, and their length was increased by some 20 inches. They were then despatched to Northern Counties at Wigan who fitted them with attractive Paladin-style single-deck bodies with 42 dual-purpose seats. This view taken outside the garage at Squires Gate on 28 May 1993 is of newly-delivered number 5 (TKU 465K). Fylde Borough Transport was sold to its management in January 1994, and five months later in the May, the business was acquired by Blackpool Transport. The base at Squires Gate was closed in 1999, and so all traces of what was originally Lytham St. Annes Corporation finally faded away.

(John Wiltshire)

In the run up to deregulation at Rossendale, it was becoming increasingly apparent that, rather than downsizing the fleet and reducing staff levels, it would be necessary to expand operations, due to the amount of new service work that it had been awarded. Several withdrawn vehicles would now need to be reinstated, and a substantial number of used buses would be required for the start of the new services. In 1989 half a dozen Atlanteans arrived from Eastbourne Buses, and having East Lancs bodies they dovetailed neatly into the Rossendale fleet. In this view we see number 130 in Manchester Piccadilly on 10 July 1991, by which time the bus was thirteen years old. The Eastbourne vehicles went on to give nearly ten years service for Rossendale.

(John Wiltshire)

Used buses were then regularly added to the Rossendale fleet, and its vehicles were now to be found working well away from its traditional territory, and serving places such as Rochdale, Bury, central Manchester and Todmorden. The last new Leyland buses to be purchased by Rossendale were a batch of four Tigers which were delivered in 1989. They were also the first order for full-size service buses since deregulation in 1986. One of them had high-backed dual-purpose type seating but the remaining three had 51 bus seats. The new quartet, numbered 92 to 95, had East Lancs bodywork, and number 93 is seen here in Bury bus station on 6 August 1990, departing for Rawtenstall. Also in view are a Leyland Atlantean and a Dodge minibus, both operating for Greater Manchester. All four Tigers were to be sold out of Rossendale ownership in 2000.

(John Jones)

The Lynx was Leyland Buses' final single-deck bus design. Launched in 1985, only one of the eight surviving Lancashire municipals at this time, Preston Borough Transport, was tempted to purchase any new Leyland Lynx. Preston actually bought fifteen examples between March 1989 and November 1990, all with Cummins L10 engines and apart from the first pair, all had 45 dual-purpose type seats. From the initial batch of four is 12 (F212 YHG), complete with high-back seats. It is seen in the depot yard when new, and would eventually be utilised on routes to the Longridge area, some six or seven miles to the north of Preston, and competing for business with private operator Mercers. In the background is an ex-Merseybus Leyland National that was new to Southport Corporation. Preston acquired four of these in 1986 primarily for use on school contracts.

(Arthur Day collection)

The main fleet livery at Hyndburn after deregulation gradually evolved to feature more red and also saw the introduction of silver bands. From their base in Accrington, Hyndburn vehicles could now be seen operating in most neighbouring towns. The last new double-deckers were a pair of Dennis Dominators in 1985, and following these, used Atlanteans were sourced from GM Buses, Plymouth and Merseybus, the latter having rather ungainly Willowbrook bodywork. Some of the last buses acquired were a smart pair of ECW-bodied Leyland Olympians from West Riding. One of these, 125 (CWR 525Y), is seen passing The Crown public house in Bacup Road, Rawtenstall, on 9 March 1995. In September 1996 Hyndburn Borough Council sold its bus operation to the Stagecoach group. The garage in Accrington was not included in the deal, and all operations were subsequently based at the Stagecoach garage in Blackburn.

(John Jones)

Preston Borough Transport introduced a very large fleet of Renault minibuses and seventeen Leyland Olympian double-deckers during the first six years of deregulation. In 1993 Preston became the subject of an employee buy-out, and later changed its title to Preston Bus Ltd. Unlike all the other employee-owned former municipal operations, Preston Bus was set to succeed and survived until 2009, and for this reason I have included it here. During this time further new vehicles were purchased including a fleet of eighteen Dennis Trident low floor double-deckers with East Lancs bodywork. Number 194 is a new example in 1999, and is seen leaving Preston bus station in January 2000. Following an intense period of competition with Stagecoach North West, the employees agreed to sell the business to the Stagecoach Group in January 2009. However, after an enquiry, Stagecoach was initially ordered to divest itself of Preston Bus. After an appeal, by the summer of 2010 an agreement was reached whereby Stagecoach would retain one former Preston Bus route, and the remaining parts would be sold off. Preston Bus was acquired by Rotala plc, with Stagecoach allowed to retain only route 11.

(A L Sutch - Andrew Wiltshire collection)

The survivors.

Only three council-owned fleets in Lancashire were destined to survive into the new millennium, and as we have seen on page 73, the Blackburn fleet would only last until 2007. It is good to see that Rossendale Transport is still with us in 2010 and serving the community in this East Lancashire borough. The fleet had grown to 113 vehicles by the summer of 2009 of which nineteen were double-deckers. Rossendale moved to new office and garage premises in Haslingden in 2008, but still retains a smaller garage, with an allocation of around forty buses, in Rochdale. Since deregulation operations have covered a much larger area than hitherto, and many buses can be found working in the Rochdale and Bury areas. Dennis Dart number 119 is seen in Accrington in March 2003, and is a 1998 delivery, one of a batch of ten with Plaxton Pointer SPD 40-seat bodywork. Subsequent fleet additions have included further Darts, Wright-bodied Volvos, several batches of 25-seat Optare Solo midi-buses and a number of second-hand double-deckers.

(Andrew Wiltshire collection)

On the Fylde coast, Blackpool Transport continues to thrive and in 2010 was in the process of upgrading its tramway with new permanent way and new trams to follow, while at the same time continuing to update its bus fleet. From 2001 until 2010 the Blackpool fleet traded as Metro Coastlines, and during this time a colour-coded route-branding system was introduced. There were over twelve such routes known as Lines. From 26 July 2010 the fleet reverted to the more familiar Blackpool Transport Services Ltd, route branding was abandoned, and a new livery was introduced. Seen in the town centre working Line 11 on 16 April 2002 is Volvo Olympian number 375, which dates from 1994, one of a batch of six similar buses with Northern Counties Palatine 2 bodies.

(John Jones)

Having passed into the county of Cheshire on 1 April 1974, the Warrington fleet was to see a change from Daimler Fleetlines to Leyland Atlanteans for its double-deck requirements. By now the livery was red and white, and from 1982 both Dennis Dominators and Leyland Olympians were purchased. After deregulation the fleet expanded considerably and many used vehicles were added to stock. The last new double-deckers arrived in 1989, but many second-hand examples like this Northern Counties-bodied Olympian number 64 (H515 RWX) joined the fleet. It is seen in Warrington on 13 November 2003, and was one of six obtained from Harrogate and District. New midi-buses and saloons formed the basis of the main fleet after 1990, with the Dennis Dart being succeeded by DAF/VDLs and more recently Volvos. In 2011 the fleet is marketed as Network Warrington.

(Andrew Wiltshire)

Widnes Corporation, having become Halton Borough Transport with the move into Cheshire, ran its last double-decker in 1979. Only saloons had been purchased since 1967, and following the purchase of Bristol RESLs many Leyland Nationals were added to the fleet. The later Nationals were Mark 2 models, and Halton took the last example built fitting it out with high-back seats. After deregulation the Leyland Lynx was popular and Halton took thirty-six including fourteen late examples in 1992. Since 1994 the Dennis Dart has reigned supreme with Marshall and later East Lancs bodywork. Delivered new in 2000, number 20 (X966 ULG) is a Marshall 8.8 metre version with seating for 28. It is seen on 1 November 2007 in unexpected surroundings, a stone's throw from the Runcorn Bridge, and in front of St Mary's church at West Bank, Widnes. This smart undertaking celebrated its centenary in 2009.

(David Beilby)